FANTASTIC FORCES

Speed and Acceleration

Richard Spilsbury

Heinemann Library
Chicago, Illinois

© 2007 Heinemann Library
a division of Reed Elsevier Inc.
Chicago, Illinois

Customer Service 888-454-2279
Visit our website at www.heinemannraintree.com

Designed by Richard Parker and Tinstar Design
    (www.tinstar.co.uk)
Printed and bound in China by WKT
    Company Limited

11 10 09 08 07
10 9 8 7 6 5 4 3 2 1

**Library of Congress Cataloging-in-Publication
Data**
Spilsbury, Richard, 1963-
    Speed and acceleration / Richard Spilsbury.
        p. cm. -- (Fantastic forces)
    Includes bibliographical references and index.
    ISBN-13: 978-1-4034-8173-3 (lib. bdg.)
    ISBN-10: 1-4034-8173-3 (lib. bdg.)
    ISBN-13: 978-1-4034-8178-8 (pbk.)
    ISBN-10: 1-4034-8178-4 (pbk.)
    1. Speed--Juvenile literature. 2. Acceleration
(Mechanics)--Juvenile literature. 3. Force and
energy--Juvenile literature. I. Title. II. Series.
    QC137.52.S65 2006
    531'.112--dc22
                                    2006002068

Acknowledgments
The publishers would like to thank the following
for permission to reproduce photographs:
Action Plus Images p. **15** (Neil Tingle); Alamy
pp. **5** (Elvele Images), **6** (Mikael Karlsson), **8**
(The Photolibrary Wales), **9** (Alaska Stock LLC),
10 (Travelshots.com), **11** (Alchemy), **14** (Visions
of America, LLC), **17** (Jeff Rotman), **21** (Buzz
Pictures), **22** (Ace Stock Limited), **24** (Gregory
Bajor), **26** (Popperfoto); Corbis pp. **13** (Peter
M. Fisher), **16**, **20** Corbis Sygma p. **23** (Seguin
Franck); Getty p. **4** (Allsport Concepts/Stu
Forster); Harcourt Education/Tudor Photography
pp. **7, 12, 18, 27**; sharkman/www.eurodragster.
com p. **19**; Science Photo Library p. **25** (Cody
Images).

Cover photograph of athlete reproduced with
permission of Digital Vision.

Picture research by Erica Newbery and Susi Paz.

Disclaimer
All the Internet addresses (URLs) given in this
book were valid at the time of going to press.
However, due to the dynamic nature of the
Internet, some addresses may have changed, or
sites may have changed or ceased to exist since
publication. While the author and publishers
regret any inconvenience this may cause readers,
no responsibility for any such changes can be
accepted by either the author or the publishers.

It is recommended that adults supervise children
on the Internet.

Contents

Speed and acceleration experiments and demonstrations

There are several experiments and demonstrations in this book that will help you to understand how speed and acceleration work. Each experiment or demonstration contains a list of the equipment you need and step-by-step instructions. You should ask an adult to help you with any sharp objects.

Materials you will use

Most of the experiments and demonstrations in this book can be done with household objects that can be found in your own home. You will also need a pencil and paper to record your results.

Any words appearing in the text in bold,
like this, are explained in the glossary.

What Is Speed?

Do you like to move fast? It can be lots of fun to cycle or run as fast as you can. **Speed** describes how fast things move.

Motion and speed

Motion is the movement of something from one place to another. If you place a soccer ball on the grass, nothing happens. It does not move. It is **stationary**. When you kick the ball, it moves. It is in motion. To make something move, you need to use a **force**. A force is a push or a pull. Forces make objects start moving, speed up, slow down, stop moving, change direction, or change shape. A force causes movement in one direction. You need to kick the ball to push it toward another player on your team or toward the goal.

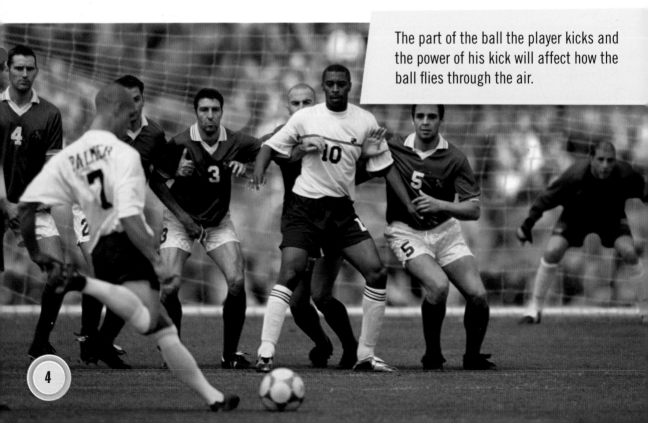

The part of the ball the player kicks and the power of his kick will affect how the ball flies through the air.

The cheetah is the fastest running animal on Earth. It needs speed to chase and catch the animals it eats.

One way to measure motion is to see how far something has moved. Imagine a slug and a rabbit racing toward a lettuce plant. The slug takes much more time to get there than the rabbit. Speed describes how long it takes for something to move a known distance in a certain time. The rabbit moves at a faster speed than the slug because it moves the same distance in less time.

Fast and slow animals

Speed is important for people. For example, we can get to school more quickly by bus than by walking. Human athletes who run or swim faster may win prizes. For animals, speed can be a matter of life or death. For example, if a rabbit cannot run to its burrow fast enough, it may get caught and killed by an owl or a fox. This table compares some of the fastest and slowest animals on the ground, in the sky, and in the sea.

Animal	Approximate miles per hour	Approximate km per hour
Peregrine falcon	200	300
Cheetah	70	110
Horse	50	80
Mako shark	45	72
Ostrich	40	65
Dragonfly	36	60
Top human sprinter	29	47
Elephant	25	40
Giant tortoise	0.2	0.3
Sloth	0.1	0.2
Snail	0.05	0.01

How do we measure speed?

We measure speed by how long something takes to travel a particular distance in a set time. For example, Jack and Ahmed both travel 1 mile (1.6 kilometers) to school by bike each day. The journey takes Jack twenty minutes and Ahmed ten minutes. Jack travels 1 mile (1.6 kilometers) in twenty minutes. Ahmed travels 1 mile (1.6 kilometers) in ten minutes. Ahmed is quicker than Jack. People usually measure distances with tape measures and rulers. They measure time using clocks and stopwatches.

Units to measure speed

Speed is measured in feet per second and miles or kilometers per hour. The word *per* means "in each." Imagine a red car travels 40 miles (60 kilometers) per hour and a blue car travels 25 miles (40 kilometers) per hour. Which is going faster? The red car is going faster. It is easy to compare the cars' speeds if we use the same **units**.

DID YOU KNOW?

Speed in water is often given in units called **knots**. Sailors used to measure boat speeds by dangling a heavy knotted rope into the water. They counted how many knots on the rope were pulled into the water during a given time period. This showed the speed of the boat.

Traffic police can check the speed of a car using a speed gun.

EXPERIMENT:

Speedy classmates!

Question: Is running faster than hopping?

Hypothesis: You are going to measure the speed of a friend hopping, and then running, over the same distance. The friend will be faster running.

Equipment: A long tape measure, chalk or a piece of string, a stopwatch, a friend, paper, and a pencil.

Experiment steps:
1. Use the tape to measure a 65-foot (20-meter) length of ground. Mark a start line at one end and a finish line at the other, using chalk or string.
2. Stand at the finish line. Ask a friend to stand at the start line.
3. Using the stopwatch, measure the time it takes your friend to hop from the start to finish line. Record your result on paper.
4. Repeat step 3 with your friend running.
5. Ask an adult to help you change both results into feet per second. Compare the results. Which was faster?

Conclusion: Your friend ran the race faster. Running is faster than hopping.

Which Forces Make Things Move?

If you sit on a bike and do nothing, you do not move. You will only move if you use a **force**. You will only move if you push against the ground or push down on the pedals. There are three main forces that make things move: **thrust**, **gravity**, and **magnetism**.

Thrust

Thrust is the name we give to a push or pull that starts movement. Animals thrust forward in several different ways. Horses push or thrust their feet against the ground to move forward. Birds start to move by flapping their wings. Their wings push or thrust against the air around them.

Fish push or thrust their tail fins up and down or side to side. Their tail fins push against the water behind them. Jellyfish take water into their flexible bodies. Then, they use their muscles to squirt it out fast. The force of this water pushing against the water around them pushes the animals forward.

Cyclists push on their pedals to make a chain turn their back wheel. The tire on the back wheel grips and pushes against the ground. This thrusts the bike forward.

Imagine the amount of power orcas need to use to thrust their heavy bodies out of the water!

People have invented many machines that thrust forward in a way that is similar to animals. For example, jet skis use engines to suck in and squirt out water in the way squids do. The engines on most airplanes do a similar thing. They force out air and hot gases made in the engine. This thrusts them forward.

Gravity

Gravity is a force that pulls every object on Earth downward. Gravity actually pulls all objects toward each other. The heavier the objects are, the bigger the pull. Earth is so big that it pulls everything on or near its surface toward its center. Without Earth's gravity, we would float up into the air. This is what happens in space.

This roller coaster moves at high **speed** down slopes because it is being pulled toward Earth by gravity.

Sometimes you can feel the gravity of very large objects. For example, some giant ships are so heavy that they will start to move toward each other if they pass too closely.

We can use gravity to move. When you step off a diving board, gravity pulls you straight down into the water. Gravity also pulls things down slopes. For example, you will not move anywhere if you are sitting on the flat part at the top of a slide. If you move onto the slope, you will slip down the slide. Slides usually flatten out at the bottom to stop you from sliding off the end and ending up on the floor! Gravity is also the force that makes roller coasters move fast.

Magnetism

Magnetism is another force that can cause movement. For example, two magnets can pull together. This pull is called **magnetic attraction**. People can use magnetic attraction to find their way with a **compass**. A compass has a moving needle inside with a magnet in its tip. Magnetic rock inside Earth attracts the magnet on the end of the needle. The needle then points toward the north. Magnets can also push away other magnets. This is called **magnetic repulsion**.

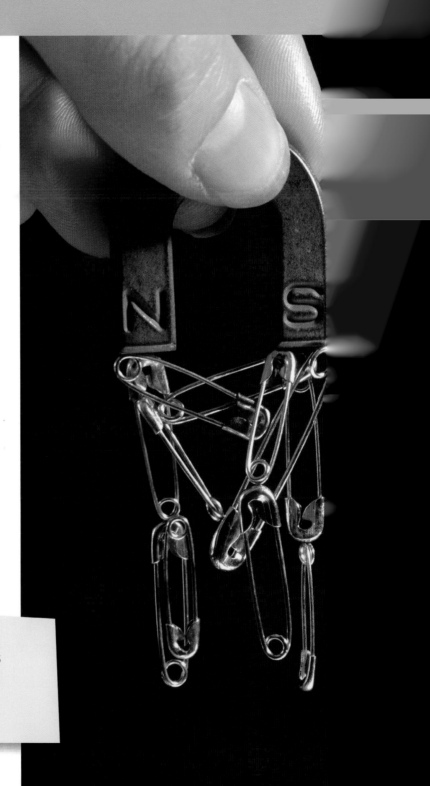

The force of magnetism has caused these safety pins to jump toward a magnet.

DEMONSTRATION:

A balloon car

This demonstrates how air squirting out of a balloon creates thrust. This thrust can move a plastic car forward.

Equipment: An empty plastic milk carton with a lid, a balloon, two straws, four spools of thread, modeling clay, scissors, and sticky tape.

Demonstration steps:

1. Cut off the milk carton handle to make a large hole in the side. Make a small hole in the lid. Ask an adult to help you.
2. Put the open end of the balloon through the hole in the lid from the inside. Do not blow it up yet. This is the car's engine!
3. Make two holes on each side of the carton and push the straws though these holes. The straws are the **axles**, which the wheels will fit on. Make sure the holes are close to the bottom so that you do not damage the balloon.
4. Put the spools of thread on the ends of the straws. Plug the ends of the straws with modeling clay, to keep the spools on. These are the wheels.
5. Now, blow up the balloon and pinch its neck.
6. Put the car down and let go of the balloon.

Explanation: When you let go of the balloon, air rushes out. The air pushes or thrusts against air behind the car and makes the car move forward.

motion

air escapes

How Do Forces
Balance Each Other?

In a tug-of-war, two teams pull on either end of a rope that has a tie in the middle. If the teams are equally strong, their pulls in opposite directions have the same strength, and the tie stays where it is.

Nothing much happens in a tug-of-war competition if the teams are evenly matched. But if one team is stronger, the forces are not balanced anymore. One team pulls the other over.

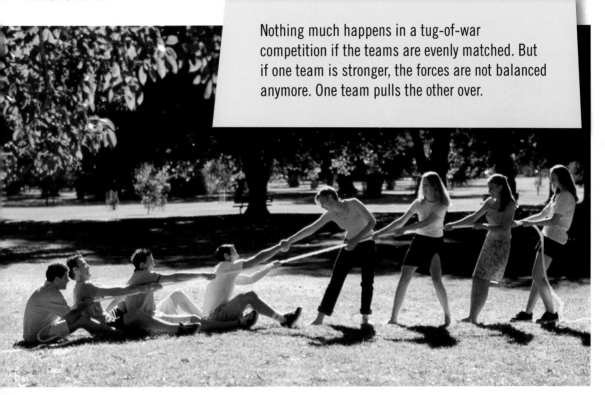

Balanced forces

Forces act in pairs. They push or pull in opposite directions. If the forces are the same strength, the object does not move. When a pair of forces does not make an object move, we say the forces are balanced. It is easy to spot when a seesaw is balanced. The **weight** of the person on either side of the seesaw is the same. The seesaw stays level.

Sometimes balanced forces are not so easy to spot. Have you ever seen a dragonfly or hummingbird flapping its wings fast to stay in one position in mid-air? The force of **gravity** pulls the animal down. The force of the air, crushed under the animal's wings as it flaps them, pushes the animal up. The force of air pushing up is called **uplift**. When the force of gravity and the force of uplift are balanced, the animal hovers in the air.

When a bumper car crashes into another bumper car, the big push unbalances the forces of the hit car. It may move faster, slow down, or change direction.

Hammer throwers train hard to build up their strength and timing. They must let go of the hammer at the right time. Otherwise, it might go crashing into the cage they spin in!

DID YOU KNOW?

Hammer throwers move their hammers in a circle. The pull of the thrower on the weight stops it from moving in a straight line. The pull makes the forces unbalanced. When the thrower lets go of the chain, the pull stops and the hammer flies off in a straight line. The forces are balanced once more.

What are unbalanced forces?

In a tug-of-war, if one team is stronger than the other, the stronger team pulls the weaker team over. The forces are unbalanced. Unbalanced forces always cause **motion** to change. Sometimes they make the direction of movement change. For example, moving marbles change direction when they crash into each other.

Which Forces Slow Things Down?

On a skateboard you would soon slow down and stop if you did not keep pushing with your foot. This is because your wheels grip the rough ground and your body pushes against the air around you. These things affect everything that moves at **speed**.

What is friction?

When two surfaces rub against each other, a **force** called **friction** slows them down. Friction happens because tiny bumps on the surfaces catch against each other. Even objects that look very smooth still have bumpy surfaces, which you can see under a microscope. However, friction is much greater on rough surfaces, such as concrete, than on smooth surfaces, such as glass.

Good and bad friction

Good friction	Example
Friction stops us from sliding on slippery surfaces	Tires on racing-car wheels
Friction helps us slow down	Brakes against a bike wheel

Bad friction	Example
Friction slows big things down	Trucks are slower than cars
Friction makes things hot	Car engines get hot and can overheat

The heaviest road vehicles, such as this timber truck, move slowly. There is a lot of friction between their large wheels and the ground. The friction slows them down.

The octopus spreads its arms wide as it drops toward its food. It pushes down many water molecules. This increases water resistance and slows down the octopus.

Friction also happens in air and water. This friction is called **drag**. For example, when an airplane flies, the air pushes against it. The force of air pushing against the airplane is called drag. When you swim through water in a swimming pool, you can feel water pushing against you. The force of water pushing against you is called drag. Drag is greater in water than in air because water is thicker than air. That is why landing in a deep pool of water stops you from moving after coming down a waterslide!

Pushing back

Drag in air is also called **air resistance**. Drag in water is also called **water resistance**. Air and water resistance slow down a moving object. Air and water are made up of tiny **particles** called **molecules**. The molecules squeeze together in front of a moving object. They then press back against the object. The faster the object moves forward, the harder the molecules press back. The faster the object moves forward, the greater the resistance. The larger the front of the moving object, the more molecules press back against it. The more molecules press back against the object, the greater the air or water resistance. Without water resistance beneath boats, **gravity** would soon sink them.

EXPERIMENT:

Controlling a fall using air resistance

Question: How do parachutes work?

Hypothesis: A parachute slows down the descent (fall) of an object.

Equipment: A spool of thread, a large handkerchief, string, and a stopwatch.

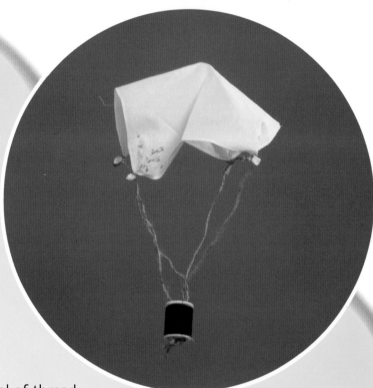

Experiment steps:

1. Ask an adult to hold the spool of thread above his or her head. Use the stopwatch to time how long it takes for the spool to hit the ground. Record the result. Then, repeat the experiment four times to see if you get a similar result each time.
2. Now, make a parachute. Tie a piece of string to each corner of the handkerchief. Poke the free end of each string through the spool of thread and tie the ends together.
3. Ask the adult to hold the spool at the same height as before with one hand. With the other hand, the adult should hold the parachute in the middle, ready for the launch. Repeat step 1.

Conclusion: The spool of thread fell more slowly with the parachute. The parachute slowed down the spool's fall.

What Is Acceleration?

A jet airplane changes **speed** on the runway from slow to very fast when it takes off. It is **accelerating**. Acceleration is the name for the change in speed. The airplane pushes out air and hot gases from its engines. The **force** of the gases pushes against the air and **thrusts** the airplane forward.

Cars accelerate when the driver pushes down on the accelerator pedal. This makes the engine burn more **fuel**. The gasoline fuel gives the car power. The extra power gives the car a bigger push or thrust. The force of **gravity** can also make moving objects accelerate downhill. For example, when you go downhill on a bicycle, you accelerate because of the force of gravity.

Dragsters are very fast cars. They accelerate to such high speeds that they need small parachutes to help them slow down.

Measuring acceleration

Acceleration is the rate of change of speed. If a race car accelerates by 90 feet per second in 3 seconds, its acceleration can be written as 30 feet per second per second!

These sprinters will thrust off their blocks at around 26 feet (8 meters) per second. To win a world-class race, they will need to accelerate to around 36 feet (11 meters) per second before crossing the line.

Feeling changes in speed

You can feel forces acting against you when a car suddenly changes speed. Have you ever felt your seat pushing into your back when a car suddenly accelerates forward? When the driver pushes hard on the brakes, you feel the opposite. Your body is pulled forward, away from the seat. In vehicles we wear seatbelts and have airbags to protect us from banging against the hard insides of the vehicle if it suddenly accelerates or **decelerates** (slows down).

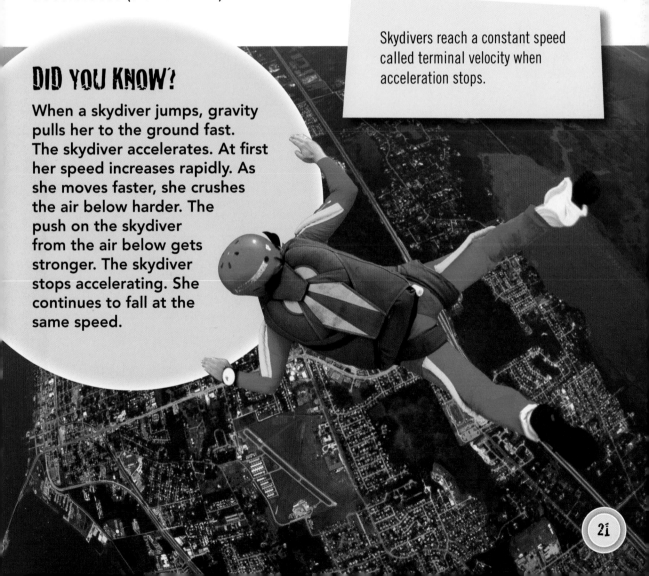

Skydivers reach a constant speed called terminal velocity when acceleration stops.

DID YOU KNOW?

When a skydiver jumps, gravity pulls her to the ground fast. The skydiver accelerates. At first her speed increases rapidly. As she moves faster, she crushes the air below harder. The push on the skydiver from the air below gets stronger. The skydiver stops accelerating. She continues to fall at the same speed.

Rides with twists, turns, and drops that make passengers feel forces several times greater than gravity are known as high-g rides.

Amusement park rides accelerate and decelerate to make passengers have fun feeling forces. For example, a passenger feels lighter on rides that suddenly drop down, such as freefall towers. Other rides use twists and turns to make passengers feel forces from the side, too.

DID YOU KNOW?

An average washing machine's spin cycle accelerates your family's wet clothes to over 160 times the force of gravity you experience just standing on Earth!

How Do People Keep Moving Fast?

People create more **thrust** to **accelerate** and reach high **speeds**. They fit vehicles with more powerful engines for extra thrust. The fastest runners train hard to develop big, strong leg muscles that can power them down the track. However, there is a limit to how strong engines and legs can get. When you cannot increase thrust any further, then the only way to go faster is to reduce the **forces** of **friction**, **air resistance**, or **water resistance** that push against the vehicle or runner.

In water

Animals such as dolphins and tuna spend their lives moving fast through water. They have **streamlined**, or smooth, shapes. The most streamlined shape is a rocket or bullet shape with a pointed tip to reduce water resistance. Top human swimmers reduce **drag** in the water by wearing swimsuits made of special material. This material makes water flow faster past them.

Top swimmers go faster by wearing full-length swimsuits that reduce drag as they move through the water.

Boats also have streamlined shapes and smooth surfaces. Some of the fastest motorboats have **hydrofoils**. These are small, streamlined wings that move under the water. They lift the boat up above the water.

In the air

High up in the sky there are strong winds that can blow against aircraft. Most modern airplanes have streamlined shapes to reduce drag in the air caused by winds. Their smooth wings are shaped to help push the aircraft up in the air as they fly forward.

DID YOU KNOW?

The fastest airplane ever built was called the SR-71. It flew 15 miles (24 kilometers) above Earth at a speed of 2,200 miles (3,500 kilometers) per hour. The SR-71 was made of special metals that did not melt in the heat caused by drag between air and its fast-moving surface. It was called the "blackbird" because it was painted black.

The wheels most aircraft need to land would slow them down once they are flying. So, they fold away to cut down on air resistance.

This *Thrust* vehicle was built just to beat the world land-speed record. It is a rocket-shaped car with aircraft jet engines attached. It has reached speeds of over 762 miles (1,227 kilometers) per hour.

On land

Skiers and snowboarders use skis and boards with smooth surfaces so there is less friction as they move over snow. They often wax the surfaces to make them even smoother. The **weight** of the skis or snowboard on the snow also melts a tiny bit of snow. This means skis and snowboards are moving on a thin layer of water. The water creates less friction than the snow.

Most land vehicles roll on wheels rather than move along on a solid bottom. As a wheel turns, only a small part touches the ground at any one time, so there is less friction. Racing bikes have much thinner tires than mountain bikes to reduce friction. This means they can go very fast.

Trains are very heavy. Most reduce friction by moving on smooth metal rails, but some use magnets. Maglev trains have strong magnets on the bottom, and there are magnets in the rail they travel on. **Magnetic repulsion** between the magnets pushes the train above the rail. Maglev trains can move faster than ordinary trains because there is no friction between the train and the rail. However, it uses a lot of electricity to make these strong magnets work.

DID YOU KNOW?

The fastest bicycle speed ever recorded is over 295 feet (90 meters) per second! However, the cyclist was riding indoors. It is easier to cycle indoors. There is less friction and air resistance. The floor is smooth and there is no wind. Outdoors, friction and air resistance push against the bicycle more and slow it down.

Speed skaters travel fast on ice using thin metal skates. The hard blades slide along on the water that melts underneath them.

EXPERIMENT:

Soap boats

Question: Which shape of boat will move faster?

Hypothesis: A streamlined boat will move faster than a blunt-shaped boat.

Equipment: Flat Styrofoam, scissors, a shallow tray of water, dish detergent, and a friend to help.

Experiment steps:
1. First, cut out two rectangular Styrofoam boats. Cut off the front corners on one boat so that its front is streamlined.
2. Cut a triangle-shaped notch in the back edge of each boat.
3. Place both boats in a line at one end of the tray of water.
4. Squirt a small drop of detergent into the water in the notch of one of the boats. Ask a friend to do the same to the other boat, at the same time.

Conclusion: The detergent will push the boats forward. The streamlined boat will move faster in the water. The streamlined boat travels easier in the water because there is less drag.

People Who Found the Answers

Galileo Galilei (1564–1642)

Galileo was an Italian scientist. There is a story that he went up to the top of Italy's Leaning Tower of Pisa and dropped metal balls of different sizes and **weights**. People thought heavier balls would fall more quickly, but Galileo saw that they landed at the same time. He realized the balls were **accelerating** at the same rate and then dropping at the same **speed** toward the ground.

Isaac Newton (1642–1727)

Newton was a very famous scientist who came up with three ideas on **motion**. He was the first to understand the importance of **forces** on speed and acceleration. He wrote that "for every action there is an equal and opposite reaction." This means that forces act in pairs. Newton watched apples falling to the ground from trees and figured out that they do this because of a force we call **gravity**.

Frank Whittle (1907–1996)

The Englishman Whittle was the son of a mechanic. When he was a young man, airplane engines had propellers to make them move. Whittle figured out how airplanes could go faster and use less **fuel**. They needed engines that blew out hot gases backward at high speed, like a rocket, to push the airplane forward. Whittle invented a jet engine. On its first test flight in 1941, the plane powered by this engine reached 340 miles (550 kilometers) per hour. This made it the fastest plane on Earth. Whittle's jet engine was further developed into the engines used in aircraft today.

Amazing Facts

- ## Fasten your seatbelt!

  The engines on a car called *Thrust*, built specially to break speed records, can produce the same **thrust** as 140 Formula One race-car engines put together. But this is tiny compared to the engines used to send the Apollo rockets into space. They can produce the same power as over 17,000 Formula One race cars!

- ## The fastest thing in the universe

  When you switch on a light in a dark room, it transforms the room in an instant. Light is the fastest thing we know of. It travels at 186,000 miles (300,000 kilometers) per second. The stars we can see twinkling on some clear nights are the lights from stars that exploded millions of years ago. They are so far away that it has taken that long for their light to reach us!

- ## Quick fliers

  Hummingbirds can beat their wings up to 200 times per second. The movement of each wing is not up and down, but rather a figure eight. They can hover and even fly backward. But this is slow flying compared to insects such as fruit flies, which can beat their wings over five times faster.

- ## High-g rides

  Riders on the fastest loop-the-loop amusement park rides feel forces three times stronger than gravity as they speed along. Riders feel very weighted down. Pilots in the fastest jet airplanes are trained to work in forces ten times greater than gravity. They have to wear special suits with built-in balloons. These press on their bodies to stop the blood from draining away from their heads when they accelerate fast up into the sky.

Glossary

accelerate increase speed over time. A bike accelerates when you pedal faster.

air resistance pushing force of air molecules against a moving object. This force increases with speed.

axle rod that wheels fit on

compass instrument that uses a magnetic needle to show direction. Magnetism is the force that makes the needle move.

decelerate decrease speed over time. A bike decelerates, or slows down, when you push on the brakes.

drag friction between a moving object and the air or water around it

force push or pull that makes an object move, accelerate, or change direction

friction force caused by contact between the surfaces of two objects. Friction slows down movement.

fuel material, such as gasoline, that is burned to give power to a machine

gravity force that pulls all objects toward the center of Earth

hydrofoil wing-like part of a boat that lifts the boat out of the water so it can travel faster

knot unit sailors use to measure boat speeds

magnetic attraction force pulling two magnets together

magnetic repulsion force pushing two magnets apart

magnetism force that makes things move using magnets

molecule tiny amount of a substance

motion movement of something from one place to another

particle a very small piece of material

speed distance an object moves in a given amount of time. For example, people can walk at a speed of about 2 miles (3 kilometers) per hour.

stationary not moving

streamlined shaped to reduce the amount of air or water resistance and drag

thrust force that makes an object move or accelerate

unit set quantity used to measure things

uplift force acting in the opposite direction from gravity

water resistance force pushing in the opposite direction from thrust in water. This force increases with speed.

weight measure of the pull of gravity on an object

Further Information

Books

Cooper, Christopher. *Science Answers: Forces and Motion.* Chicago: Heinemann Library, 2004.

Mason, Paul. *Fusion: Roller Coaster!* Chicago: Raintree, 2007.

Oxlade, Chris. *Hands-On Science: Physics: 50 Great Science Experiments and Projects.* Lanham, Md.: Southwater, 2003.

Parker, Steve. *Tabletop Scientist: Forces.* Chicago: Heinemann Library, 2006.

Solway, Andrew. *10 Experiments Your Teacher Never Told You About: Gravity.* Chicago: Raintree, 2006.

Websites

Here are a few websites you can visit to learn more or test your knowledge about fantastic forces:

Enter the world of amusement parks and look at the forces involved in some of the rides. You can even design a roller coaster! *http://www.learner.org/exhibits/parkphysics/*

Learn a little more about motion and some of the important thinkers whose ideas we use today, such as Newton and Galileo, at *http://library.thinkquest.org/11924/motion.html*

Index